BEETHOVEN
SELECTED PIANO WORKS

Edited and Recorded by Matthew Edwards

To access companion recorded performances online, visit:
www.halleonard.com/mylibrary

Enter Code
2977-2021-5682-5858

On the cover:
A Wedding Procession in the Bavarian Tyrol
by Riefstahl (W.L.)
(1827–1888)

ISBN 978-0-634-09906-9

G. SCHIRMER, Inc.

DISTRIBUTED BY

HAL•LEONARD®
CORPORATION
7777 W. BLUEMOUND RD. P.O. BOX 13819 MILWAUKEE, WI 53213

www.musicsalesclassical.com
www.halleonard.com

CONTENTS

HISTORICAL NOTES

The nearly mythical figure of Beethoven looms as large today as it did in his own century. No one has dominated his own musical milieu in quite the same way as Beethoven; no one has inspired and intimidated as many composers for as long a period as Beethoven; and certainly no other composer accomplished all of this while lacking his hearing, unarguably a musician's most important sense.

Beethoven realized he was becoming deaf in his early 30s after years of prominence in the Viennese music scene. He had moved to Vienna from his hometown of Bonn in 1792 at the age of 22. Initially he studied composition with Joseph Haydn and other distinguished composers. Three years after his arrival, he carefully orchestrated his public debut by timing the publication of his first several opus numbers with the premiere performance of a piano concerto (likely *Concerto No. 1*, the second one he had in fact written). The success of this initial flurry established Beethoven as an extraordinary musical presence virtually from the outset, and he remained an honored, albeit eccentric, celebrity in Vienna for the rest of his life.

Although born into a modest family of musicians, Beethoven moved in aristocratic circles by virtue of his genius. Members of the Viennese nobility comprised some of the more musically sophisticated patrons in all of Europe, and they commissioned dozens of works from Beethoven. For these commissions, the patron would specify the genre and the difficulty for each piece, and Beethoven could be as creative as he desired within the technical parameters. The two parties agreed on a period of time (six months, or a year, say) when the patron had exclusive rights to perform but not circulate the work, after which Beethoven was free to publish it. Beethoven prospered from these commissions and subsequent publications, living essentially without financial worry until his death in 1827.

For any great artist, music is not merely a means of feeding oneself, though such necessities are too easily discounted when we consider a life 200 years later. Acutely aware of his ambition for artistic greatness, Beethoven needed to convince publishers to rally behind his more difficult works in order to fulfill his artistic destiny. When Beethoven published a work he considered musically significant, he would assign an opus number to it. On more than one occasion, such works might have lacked immediate public appeal and money-making potential, so Beethoven would often induce publishers to produce these pieces by promising additional, less challenging works to be published without an opus number (abbreviated WoO in German). Sometimes Beethoven offered several works—both with and without an opus—as a package deal to a publisher.

Once a piece was ready for publication, Beethoven (or his representative) negotiated a contract that often involved a single fee for the work. The payment of royalties—additional money based on the number of copies sold—did not enter into the transaction, in part because the work would likely be pirated by a rival publisher within a couple of weeks. Given the financial risks of piracy, Beethoven wisely provided incentives, through his WoO works, to print the more daring works for which profits would have been less assured.

Of the two distinct categories of Beethoven's output—those with opus numbers and those without—this volume draws largely from the latter. In many cases, the pieces in the WoO category present an excellent introduction to performing Beethoven, particularly since most listeners know of Beethoven's greatness first and foremost through his more famous, numbered works.

—*Denise Pilmer Taylor*

PERFORMANCE NOTES

Beethoven's greatest works hold a prominent and lasting place in the concert repertoire, yet nestled beneath the larger works for which he is most often lauded is a substantial collection of shorter works that he crafted throughout his career. Many of the miniatures included in this edition display the same careful writing and attention to detail as his larger works. Beethoven wrote several of them for teaching purposes, as in the case of the Opus 119 Bagatelles.[1] Indeed, many of these smaller works have become well-known due to their frequent appearance in student anthologies and recital repertoire. As I sifted through more than 150 of Beethoven's shorter works for piano solo, my desire to include some well-known pieces alongside others that are lesser known guided my selections for this introductory edition. I hope that those pianists who use this edition will appreciate finding some familiar favorites, and will enjoy discovering new delights as well.

The Score and the Recording

I have suggested tempos for each piece in these prefatory notes rather than in the score. Printed metronome markings at the beginning of any score can powerfully influence a performer, even when they are clearly the editor's choice. Tempo choices, like dynamics and articulation, have considerable effect on the character of a piece and therefore rightly remain a personal decision for the individual player to make.

The recordings included with this book reflects my own interpretive preferences and personality and, as with all performances, this particular performance is one choice out of many possible ones. On another day I might have chosen to interpret these charming dances in an entirely different way. Nonetheless, the recording does reflect an informed interpretation, and may serve as a performance model for those who may need one. I hope the listener will find my performances of these works informative, inspiring, and enjoyable.

Characteristics of the Individual Works

A brief glance at the table of contents reveals that this is primarily a book of dances—only the two Bagatelles and the Sonatina fall outside this category. It is therefore important to the performer to have at least a general understanding of the characteristics of these dances to interpret them with the appropriate style.

The **Ländler's** origins date back to Austria in the late 1600s. Derived quite literally from the word "land," it is a country, or folk dance. The meter is always 3/4, but the tempo can be slow or fast. The dance's rustic nature, emphasized by stomping and hopping steps, finds its equivalent in the stylized piano solos by frequent appearances of *sforzando* markings and accents. Additionally, a frequent emphasis on the weak beats of the measure rather than the downbeat further contributes to their roughhewn, robust style. A Ländler typically follows a simple harmonic structure, rarely straying far from I, IV, and V chords.

The **Ecossaise**, a dance in 2/4 meter, was popular in Europe and England in the 18th and 19th centuries. It was a moderate to fast-tempo dance, in which couples formed two lines and then moved gradually to the top of the line as they performed the steps of the dance.

The **Contredance** is quite similar to the Ecossaise, but its origins are English.

The **German Dance** refers to the most general type of dance and its stylized counterpart found in Beethoven's shorter works for piano solo. Generally, these pieces are in 3/4 meter and are characterized by a strong downbeat coupled with a fairly quick tempo. These factors result in a forward-moving, energetic style.

The **Menuet (Minuet)** is a dance for two partners. Usually, a solitary couple danced the Menuet while others in attendance looked on. Its moderately paced tempo, 3/4 meter, and refined style reflect the courtly origins of this stately dance, the most elegant of all the pieces included in this edition.

Beethoven wrote three sets of **Bagatelles**: Opus 33 dates from 1801, Opus 119 from 1820, and Opus 126 from 1824. As mentioned previously, Beethoven used these piano solos as teaching material for his students. The Bagatelles Opus 119 and 126 were written in close proximity to the composition of his last piano sonata, Opus 111, and the *Missa Solemnis*. They are striking for their attention to detail and exhibit Beethoven's transcendent, mature style. Beethoven may have relished the opportunity to focus on smaller forms in writing these exquisite miniatures as a kind of respite from the formidable effort of creating these other, monumental works.

The **Sonatina in G Major** is a well-known pedagogical work, one of several sonatinas by Beethoven that were undoubtedly written for his students. Its first movement reflects a basic *sonata-allegro* form, and therefore serves as an appropriate preview of its larger siblings, the 32 sonatas. In the sonatina, students can readily observe the divisions and harmonic structure of this important three-part form: Exposition, Development and Recapitulation; it even contains a very brief coda, a formal element whose role Beethoven considerably augmented in his sonatas. In his catalogue of Beethoven's works, Georg Kinsky notes the slight possibility that Beethoven did not actually write this sonatina, but tradition has ascribed it to him nonetheless.

Some General Observations

The more detailed notes for each work present several recurring ideas regarding the performance of these dances, in particular, concepts related to line, multi-voice writing, and variation. I've outlined these ideas below first, as they pertain to all the works. More detailed comments for each work may be found in the section titled "The Individual Works."

Line

The Classical era emphasized order and balanced proportion in phrasing and form. Motives are the building blocks for themes; the theme and the harmonic structure define the phrase; phrases combine to form periods; and periods organize the larger form as a whole. The performer must consider each of these structural points when making a dynamic plan for a work. The number of measures in a phrase, as well as the chords upon which they close, will guide one's interpretive choices. For example, a half cadence on the dominant typically feels inconclusive, and the dynamic choice should coincide with that feeling. Also, cadence points within phrases are common, and must be treated musically as part of the larger line. I caution the performer to avoid a sense of closure each time a phrase ends. In particular, the final conclusion of the line should come at the end of the period, with earlier phrase endings considered in the light of this ultimate goal. Taken a step further, the performer should consider even these periodic endings within the scope of the entire work. Beethoven's shorter works and dances afford students an excellent opportunity to study these principles, and can lead them to a broader perspective concerning the dynamic and musical architecture of much larger works in general.

Multiple Voices

For the sake of simplicity, I use the term "polyphony" to describe phrases in which at least one notable secondary melody accompanies the primary melodic idea. These secondary melodic lines may be long or short, and may occur as single-note lines in one hand or the other:

German Dance in C Major, WoO 8, No. 7: mm. 21-23

or as upper and lower voices in one single hand. For example:

Menuet in B-flat Major, WoO 7, No. 8: mm. 9-10

This latter kind of polyphony can be the most satisfying for both performer and listener, for it often occurs as a bit of a surprise, particularly if the line is hidden within a progression of chords or intervals, as shown here:

German Dance in G Major, WoO 8, No. 6: mm. 1-4

Voicing these lines carefully will help to bring them out clearly to the listener's ear.

Variation

Because they are derived from simple folk dances, these short works, particularly the Ländler, often contain a great deal of repetition. In Baroque music, when an entire section of any work is repeated, the standard performance practice is to vary the repeat, at least by ornamenting the line. The same is true for Classical-period music, but to a lesser degree. As discussed above in reference to musical line, many of the melodies in these dances contain similar motives and phrases. Occasionally, the only difference between one phrase and the next is whether the line cadences on the dominant or the tonic, and so the risk of sounding repetitious is an issue that must be resolved. The performer must provide sufficient variety throughout the piece by using varied dynamics and articulation in the repeats of larger sections, and by playing similar motives within each phrase with subtle distinctions in touch, tone, or articulation.

Beethoven did not always indicate detailed interpretive directions in these shorter works. In fact, he was remarkably inconsistent when it came to writing in details such as slurs, articulation, and so forth. A few have quite specific interpretive markings throughout; others begin with much detail, but the indications then trail off to nothing, sometimes after only the first phrase. In such instances, we may assume that the articulation indicated at the outset applies to similar phrases throughout the piece.

Some common ways to distinguish repeated motives within a phrase are to play the repeated element softer, as an echo effect, or to vary the articulation, playing one motive *staccato* and the next *legato*. However, for some of these works, the performer will need to work variety in through more subtle effects without distracting too much from the overall line. The notes for the individual works suggest various ways to achieve variety through dynamics, articulation, or the use of expressive *rubato*.

The Individual Works

Ländler in D Major, WoO 15, No. 2

Tempo: ♩ = 168

This dance is distinguished by its nimble, alternating *legato* and *staccato* touches in the right-hand melody. This challenge may call for some preliminary technical work. I suggest practicing scales or arpeggios in two to four octaves, ascending and descending, alternating between *legato* and *staccato* touches in groups of three to four notes each. It may suffice to practice this exercise only with the right hand, since the left hand does not need to master this feat of dexterity. However, practicing these alternating touches hands together may strengthen overall agility and help the performer to acquire a controlled, conscious *staccato* touch—one that does not sound accented or punched. The B section's success depends on playing it with one long *crescendo* from beginning to end. Be aware of exactly how many measures it will take to reach *f* so that you don't arrive there too soon.

Ecossaise in E-flat Major, WoO 86

Tempo: ♩ = 126-138

Play this simple, elegant dance in a style that will emphasize the gracefulness of the treble writing. The chords in the bass effectively establish the 2/4 meter, but by no means should they overshadow the melody by becoming accented or heavy. Despite the *sforzando* markings, a measured *crescendo* in the right hand will keep the focus on the ultimate goal of this line—the B-flat half note in measure 4. With this larger goal in place, the rest of the dance falls naturally into regular, four-bar phrases.

Ländler in D Minor, WoO 15, No. 4

Tempo: ♩ = 152

Repetitive works such as this call on the performer to experiment with different ways of playing the same material, so that it always sounds fresh and new. Some obvious possibilities for variation include a dynamic echo, or a "reverse echo" (*p–f*); a change in the articulation; or a change in the tonal quality of the motive.

Keep the left-hand dynamic level appropriately under that of the right hand, particularly so in the A section where it serves as the percussive element of the dance. Note the subtle instance of polyphony in the B section, mm. 9-15, between the right-hand melody and the hint of a countermelody in the left-hand thirds. This polyphony could be emphasized in performance as yet another source of variation.

Ecossaise in G Major, WoO 23

Tempo: ♩ = 120

Two prominent non-harmonic tones—the treble E in measure 2 and the treble A♯ in measure 4, define this work, contributing greatly to its playful, almost humorous character.

Ecossaise in G Major, WoO 23: mm. 1-4

Remember, though, that these dissonances are not isolated events, but part of a longer line. They may indeed warrant accents, but over-emphasizing them would break up the melodic line. Think beyond the dissonance to the melodic line that follows.

In the middle section (mm. 9-12), the repetition of the opening idea provides an opportunity for dynamic variation. Keeping the tempo steady, with no *ritard* whatsoever to the very end, brings this piece to an abrupt, effective conclusion, adding yet another surprise for the listener.

Ländler in D Major, WoO 11, No. 2

Tempo: ♩ = 160

The A section has a natural four-bar rise followed by a four-bar descent. Use this to help carry the musical line over the rests rather than letting them break up the phrase. The middle section, mm. 8-16, presents a good opportunity to observe how simple harmonic tension can help determine

dynamic direction. This section moves temporarily to A major, and uses only dominant and tonic chords. The melody is nothing more than arpeggiated chords, so our dynamic choices must be based solely on the tension of the dominant (*crescendo*) and its ultimate release (*decrescendo*) into the tonic.

Ländler in D Major, WoO 11, No. 2: mm. 16-21

German Dance in C Major, WoO 8, No. 1

Tempo: ♩ = 192

As in several other dances in this collection, I have chosen a faster tempo here to accentuate the pulse of the downbeat. This has the effect of "lifting" the rhythm, causing it to be brighter and lighter. Choosing a slower tempo may work, but I would suggest moving it down only to about 138—again, without overemphasizing the quarter notes, which would cause this piece to sound heavy and pedantic. The interesting accompanimental line in mm. 7-8 is notable: bringing this small motive out slightly complements the right-hand line nicely. In the recording, you will hear rolled chords in the repeat of the B section—a simple variant that Beethoven would surely have welcomed.

Ländler in D Major, WoO 11, No. 4

Tempo: ♩ = 160

The Ländler in WoO 11 were originally scored for violin and cello. This fact is good to keep in mind, particularly when playing the B section of this dance. One can almost hear a violin articulating the quite disjunct right-hand melody, while the cello provides harmonic support on the lower intervals. Imitating these instruments will help evoke the proper sound. Also, find every occasion for dynamic variety, as the melodic elements in this dance frequently repeat, unchanged. There may be merit in varying the articulation in certain places, such as at m. 12, where playing all the eighth notes *staccato* might be a better choice.

German Dance in B-flat Major, WoO 13, No. 2

Tempo: ♩. = 72

An exercise in contrasts, this dance moves swiftly from strong *marcato* chords to delicate slurred lines, and from *forte* octaves to a lyrical, ornamented melody. Whatever the mood, the tempo should be brisk enough to make the dotted-half note the underlying pulse. The parallel 6ths between the hands in the trio will be heard best if the right-hand dynamic is only slightly louder than the left.

Additionally, both hands are assigned to play the F in measure 23. I recommend that both hands should, indeed, play this note in order to maintain the continuity of each line. Measures 25-28 sound more reflective than the other sections; a slight *ritard* may enhance that quality even further.

German Dance in G Major, WoO 8, No. 6

Tempo: ♩ = 184

Playing this dance with a conscious emphasis on each quarter note throughout the A section will give it an appropriately rustic character. In mm. 9-12, be sure to voice the top notes and also begin *f*, not *ff* as marked, thereby allowing for a long *crescendo* to the last beat of measure 12, making the line musical, not simply percussive. The lyrical character of the trio contrasts greatly to the preceding section. De-emphasizing the quarter-note pulse here and shaping the melodic idea across four measures, rather than just two, will enhance its lyrical style. The absence of slurs in the A section and their multiple appearances in the B section give further support to the quite different musical characters of these two sections. This striking contrast makes this particular dance very appealing and also engages the listener's attention quite readily.

German Dance in C Major, WoO 8, No. 7

Tempo: ♩. = 66-69

This dance opens with a wonderful *legato* study for both hands. The right-hand, eighth-note melody should be played *molto legato* with careful finger control, and it must float effortlessly over the accompanying chords. Keeping those left-hand chords *legato* as well is a slightly trickier task. Using pedal here is not an option, as it would blur the right-hand melody. Rather than instinctively pedaling each downbeat, a better way to connect the chords is to let the keys rise only enough for the hammers to fall back in preparation for the next chord, causing the dampers never to make full contact with the strings. Careful practice of this rather subtle touch can yield a beautiful result, and will also produce a very liquid *legato* in the right hand. The emphatic broken-octave rumblings in mm. 25-28 display the stormy side of Beethoven, and should be played accordingly and in great contrast to the piano section that follows immediately in mm. 29-32.

German Dance in G Major, WoO 8, No. 11

Tempo: ♩. = 69

This work can be performed successfully at two different tempos. However, whether a moderate tempo (♩ = 168) or a quick one (♩. = 69) is chosen, feeling the pulse correctly is most important. At a moderate tempo, a quarter-note pulse predominates, and the dance takes on a sort of heavy, rustic character. One might imagine a dance with a more complex set of steps in this case. At the quicker pace, the dotted-half note becomes the underlying pulse, and the phrases fall naturally into longer, four-bar phrases, rather than two, and the dotted-half note becomes the pulse. Focusing on the longer phrases will keep the piece from sounding breathless in the faster tempo. As always, the grace notes here should be played gracefully, and not with a phrase-breaking accent.

Ländler in D Major, WoO 11, No. 7

Tempo: ♩ = 168

In my opening comments I mentioned that these dances often lack consistent interpretive markings, such as slurs and *staccatos*. This Ländler provides an excellent opportunity to explore the various interpretive possibilities afforded by the scarcity of markings. Detailed articulations appear at the beginning of the piece, but are missing from subsequent, similar measures. For example, in mm. 3 and 4 (and similar passages in the Coda), the articulation is indicated very precisely, but the same figure, just three measures later, has none.

Ländler in D Major, WoO 11, No. 7: mm. 3-5 and mm. 7-8, r.h.

The same inconsistency occurs in the Coda, where the articulation is indicated clearly in mm. 32-33, but is missing from the same figure in mm. 34-35.

Ländler in D Major, WoO 11, No. 7: mm. 32-36, r.h.

In these cases, it might be reasonable to conclude that Beethoven, or perhaps his publisher, forgot to mark in the articulations, especially since the rest of the piece contains detailed interpretive marks. Therefore, it makes perfect sense to apply the same articulation to similar passages.

The omissions that present more of a puzzle for the performer occur in mm. 11-12, 18-20, and in mm. 37-40. Here, the performer has no comparable passages to use as a reference, and so must make an independent decision about the kind of articulation to apply to these phrases, based on the surrounding phrases and overall character of the piece. While the ambiguity of these measures may present some vexing moments for performers, they may also provide fertile material for an imaginative solution.

This Ländler is also notable for its extended coda, which exemplifies Beethoven's penchant for writing a coda that is longer than any other single section of the whole work. In this case, the coda is longer than the main body of this short piece.

Structurally, a coda can serve as a reiteration or elaboration of the main themes of a work. Here, Beethoven only hints at the original ideas: mm. 29-31 seem to allude to mm. 3 and 4; mm. 36 and 38 repeat a prominent rhythmic figure—a quarter note followed by a half note—found in the opening section. This rhythmic figure is common to Ländlers in general, and is not unique to this piece. Harmonically, the coda is fairly static, its few chord changes masked by a constant D pedal tone. The performer's responsibility then, is to create the most interesting right-hand line possible, spinning out long phrases in the passagework, punctuated by a few surprise *sforzandos*.

Bagatelle in A Minor, Opus 119, No. 9

Tempo: ♩ = 184

This brief, graceful waltz, perhaps the most beautiful work in this book, presents many

challenges for the intermediate performer. In the fingerings, you will see that the right-hand eighth note E in measure 1 is assigned to finger 2, but the thumb is also given in parenthesis as an alternate fingering.

Bagatelle in A Minor Opus 119, No. 9: mm. 1-2, r.h.

Those with smaller hands should clearly choose the thumb, and possibly even use it again for the second eighth note in measure 2. But when the second finger plays this note, it becomes readily apparent that the entire arpeggiated figure consists of two four-note chords in succession: a first-inversion A minor chord, followed by a root-position A minor chord.

Bagatelle in A Minor, Opus 119, No. 9: mm. 1-2, r.h.

Therefore, using the second finger in measure 1 allows the performer to make only one position change for the figure—not counting the final E and C—as opposed to three position changes when the thumb is used in measure 1. Both fingerings work, and the performer should choose the one that elicits the most graceful sound. The bass-note downbeats throughout should be supportive, but never heavy.

Contredance in C Major, WoO 14, No. 1

Tempo: ♩ = 126

This lively dance's left-hand accompaniment figure affords the student a great introductory exercise in double-note tremolos. Maintaining speed and clarity in these 16th-note passages provides ample challenge to the performer, but keeping this busy, energetic accompaniment under control as well, so that it does not overwhelm the melody, is equally important.

I have suggested a fairly fast tempo for this piece so that the strong quarter-note pulse propels the line forward. A slower tempo can also work, however. Choosing a tempo as slow as ♩ = 88 will give the dance a bouncier, less driving sound. At this pace, the eighth note becomes the basic rhythmic pulse. At either tempo, this joyous dance should be played with excitement and great energy. Beethoven's use of the half cadence and binary form also makes this an excellent instructional piece to show the integral relationship between harmony and form.

Menuet in B-flat Major, WoO 7, No. 8

Tempo: ♩ = 100

This lovely menuet presents some good musical challenges; technically speaking, it is the most difficult dance in this collection. In the A section, one must again be attentive to the melodic accompaniment in the left hand, particularly the pitches that fall on the main beats in each measure. In mm. 9-12, the polyphony becomes more obvious, with two separate lines in the right hand accompanied by a third line in the left. In addition to careful voicing, if one contrasts the articulation of the two right-hand lines, they will sound more distinct.

In the Trio, the challenge becomes a more technical one because of the frequent repeated notes. It is common to play each repeated note with a different finger, e.g. 4,3,2,1, etc. For most of these instances, however, I have chosen to play each group of repeated notes with the same finger. This fingering choice won't be successful if the hand (or arm) sinks to the bottom of the key bed. Rather, the hand must make a sort of small forward motion on the keys, rising as it reaches the end of the group. This helps to retain control over the beauty and consistency of the sound, rather than relinquishing that control by changing fingers—an action that typically causes the fingers to pull away from the keyboard, and essentially away from the sound!

Sonatina in G Major, Kinsky-Halm Anh. 5, No. 1

First Movement: Moderato

Tempo: ♩ = 144-152

Although Kinsky notes that this work is "probably spurious," tradition attributes it to Beethoven. Indeed, this well-crafted sonatina deserves its prominent place in pedagogical repertoire even if its true author may be in doubt.

The sparse interpretive markings in this work again provide the performer with a range of choices regarding dynamic shaping, articulation, and phrasing. Many possibilities exist that would bring about an effective, stylistic performance. It is only important to observe the few slurs and articulations that are indicated in these movements, and then create a complete interpretation starting from these basic indications. For example, in the first movement, mm. 12-14, the descending lines in the right hand and the ascending line in m. 15 could be played either *legato* or *staccato*, or even a combination of the two articulations.

Sonatina in G Major: first movement, mm. 12-15, r.h.

This restrained editorial style does ask the performer to take more responsibility for these decisions, but I am confident that most performers and students will arrive at a tasteful interpretation even without detailed guidance, provided that they know enough about the style of the period and have listened to many fine performances of this kind of music.

The form of the first movement bears a resemblance to *sonata-allegro* form, although it does stray from the textbook version of that form in two notable ways: it is monothematic and adheres firmly to the tonic key rather than modulating to the dominant. Students learning this work will undoubtedly benefit from a formal analysis of this sonatina, however brief. Despite its departure in places from standard sonata form, or perhaps because of them, it provides an excellent introduction to the formal concepts of ternary form and *sonata-allegro* form.

The tempo I have suggested for this movement will ensure that the movement retains a bright but unhurried character. The performer should always be aware of subtle lines in the left-hand accompaniment—for example, the top notes in mm. 3-4, or the top notes in mm. 13-15. Giving these lines some melodic emphasis will deepen the expressive character of the movement.

Second Movement: Romanza

Tempo: ♩. = 80

A "Romanza" may be played at a slower tempo than the one marked here. However, remember that tempo indications are generally relative to the pulse of the music, and in a 6/8 meter such as this one, it is the dotted-quarter note—not the eighth note—that serves as the true pulse. At the very least, this idea should serve as a caution not to set the tempo so slow that the musical lines break or become difficult to shape. In my view, ♩. = 63 is the slowest workable tempo.

There is room for a bit of drama in this movement, seen first in mm. 18-21, as the right hand holds the E and then wanders leisurely back to the main theme, almost like a non-measured, operatic *recitative*. Another expressive moment is found at mm. 30-31, where the music becomes almost reflective and reminiscent; using *poco rubato* here will convey that sentiment aptly.

Bagatelle in A Major, Opus 119, No. 4

Tempo: ♩ = 60

With its detailed melodic accompaniment in the left hand and delicate inner voices, this Bagatelle is the most nearly polyphonic piece in the book. The performer must take care to shape all three lines, shifting the focus from one to another as the opening phrases repeat.

The *Andante cantabile* tempo Beethoven assigns to this piece aptly describes the exquisitely lyrical nature of this beautiful solo, and the 16th notes in the B section emphasize the need for a slower tempo throughout. They should be played at an unhurried pace so that they contribute to the reflective mood of the work. Observe the two-note slurs precisely, but without a sharp, *staccato* release of the second note, so that each passage still sounds nearly *legato*.

Some Final Thoughts

In the year 1812, Beethoven was arguably the most well-known and important composer on the European continent. By his 42nd year, he had completed eight symphonies, all of the piano concertos, all but the last six piano sonatas, and he stood poised on the brink of the most introspective and daring compositional period of his life. Yet in the midst of these formidable accomplishments and the lofty status granted him by an adoring public, he wrote a letter of a most personal nature. It is not the famous "Immortal Beloved" letter, which dates from the same year; rather, it is a brief reply to a young girl named Emilie. To show her admiration for the great composer, Emilie, who was probably nine or ten years old, had sent Beethoven a pocketbook that she had embroidered. Among the lines of his reply are these words:

> "…*Your pocketbook will be treasured among other tokens of a regard that many people have shown me but that I am still far from deserving.*
>
> *Persevere, do not only practice your art, but endeavor also to fathom its inner meaning; it deserves this effort. For only art and science can raise men to the level of gods.*"[2]

I trust that these brief lines penned by Beethoven himself will be a source of encouragement and inspiration to all musicians, young and old alike.

—*Matthew Edwards*

Notes

1. Lockwood, Lewis. *Beethoven: The Music and the Life.* New York: W.W. Norton & Co., 2003.

2. Shedlock, J. S., trans. and ed. *Beethoven's Letters.* New York: Dover Publications, 1972.

References

Rosen, Charles. *The Classical Style: Haydn, Mozart, Beethoven.* exp. ed. New York: W. W. Norton, 1997.

_____. *Sonata Forms.* rev. ed. New York: W. W. Norton, 1988.

Shedlock, J. S., trans. and ed. *Beethoven's Letters.* New York: Dover Publications, 1972.

Solomon, Maynard. *Beethoven.* 2nd rev. ed. New York: Schirmer Trade Books, 1998.

Ländler in D Major

Ludwig van Beethoven
WoO 15, No. 2

Ecossaise in E-flat Major

Ludwig van Beethoven
WoO 86

Ländler in D Minor

Ludwig van Beethoven
WoO 15, No. 4

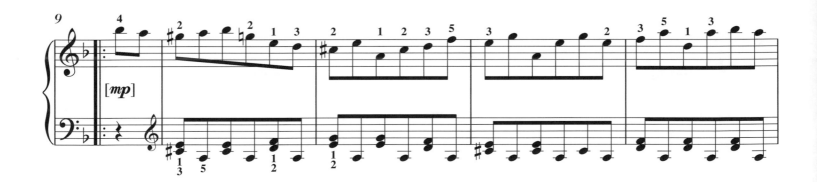

Ecossaise in G Major

Ludwig van Beethoven
WoO 23

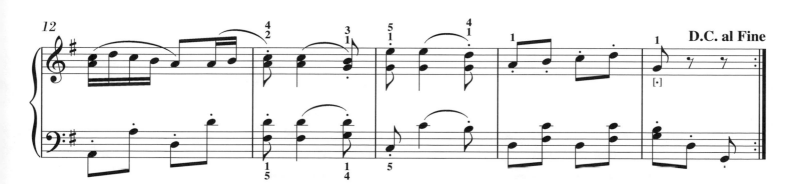

Ländler in D Major

Ludwig van Beethoven
WoO 11, No. 2

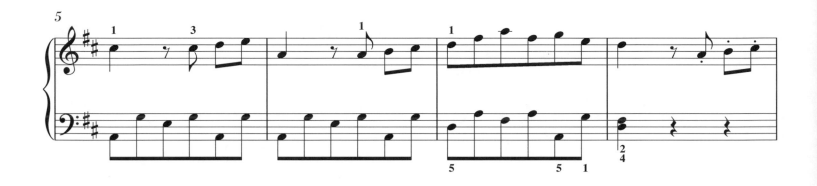

German Dance in C Major

Ludwig van Beethoven
WoO 8, No. 1

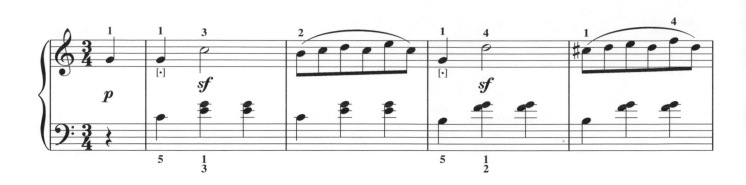

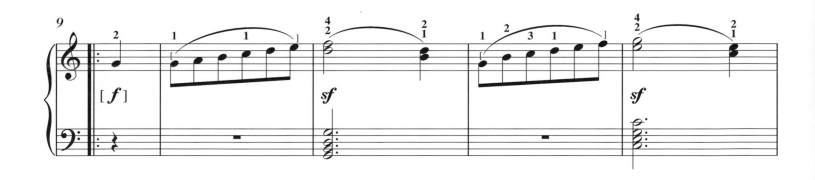

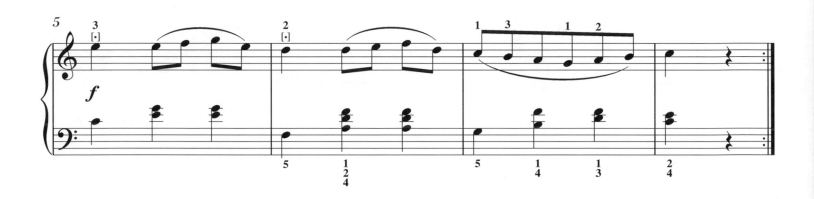

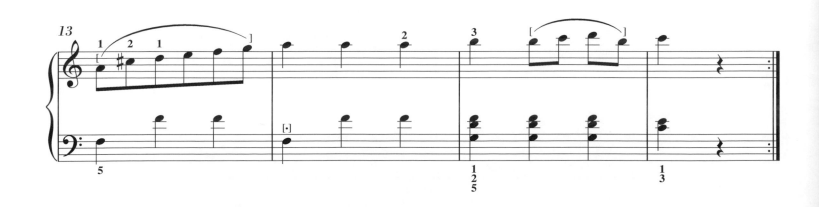

Ländler in D Major

Ludwig van Beethoven
WoO 11, No. 4

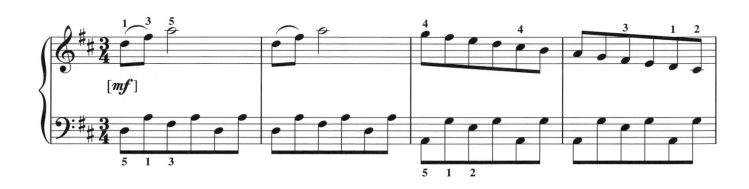

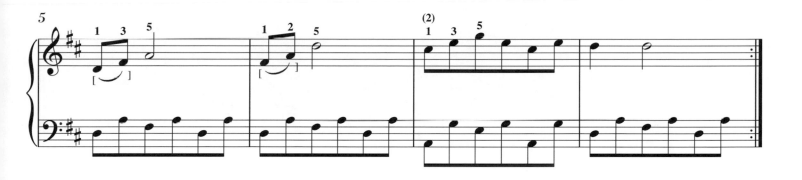

German Dance in B-flat Major

Ludwig van Beethoven
WoO 13, No. 2

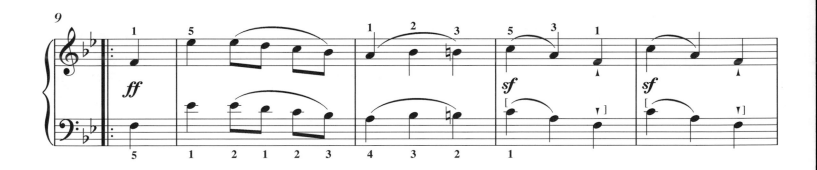

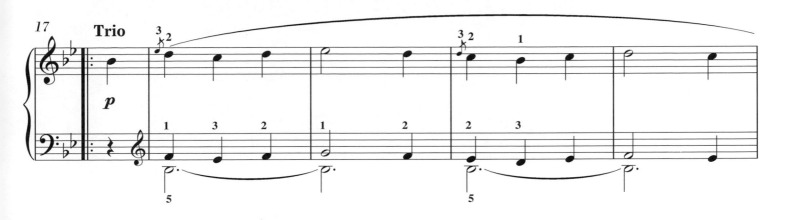

Trio

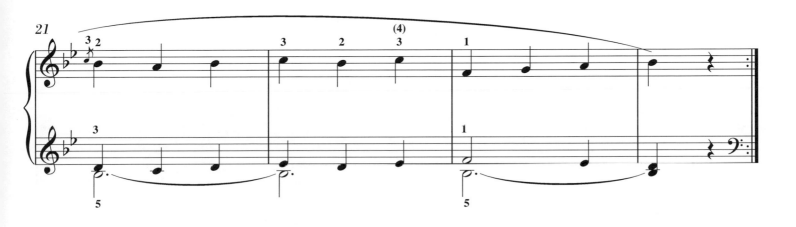

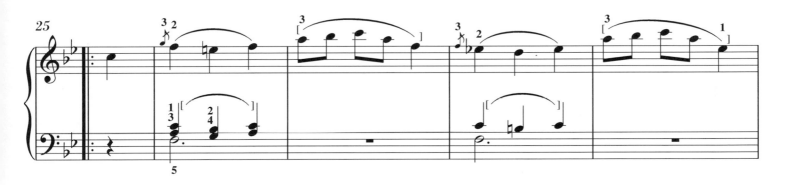

D.C. al Fine
senza repetizione

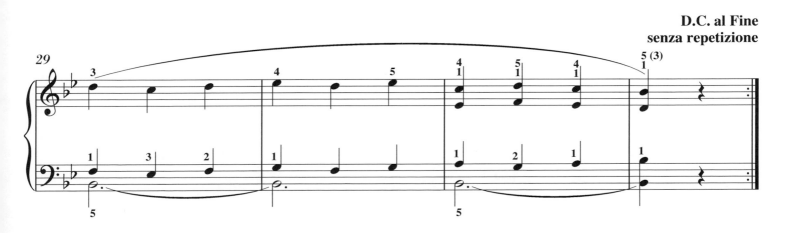

German Dance in G Major

Ludwig van Beethoven
WoO 8, No. 6

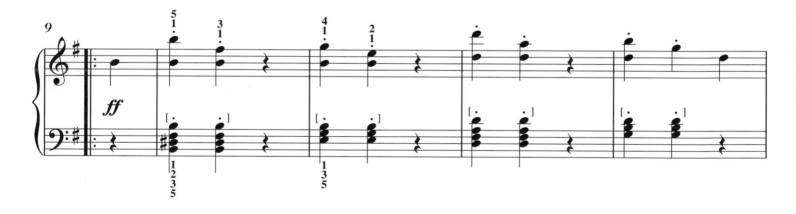

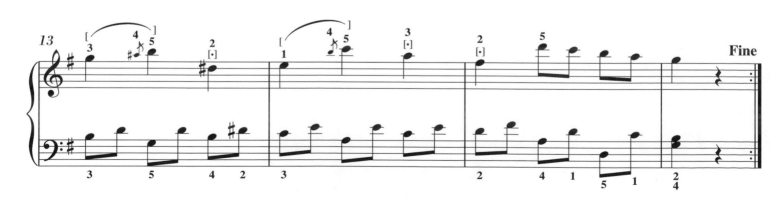

Trio

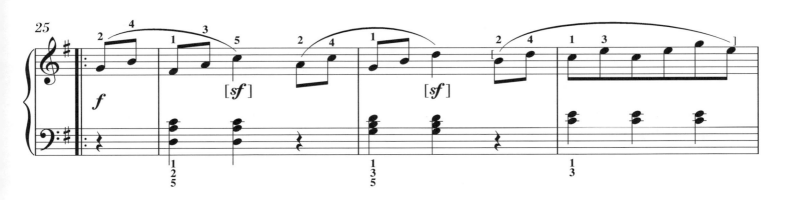

D.C. al Fine
senza repetizione

German Dance in C Major

Ludwig van Beethoven
WoO 8, No. 7

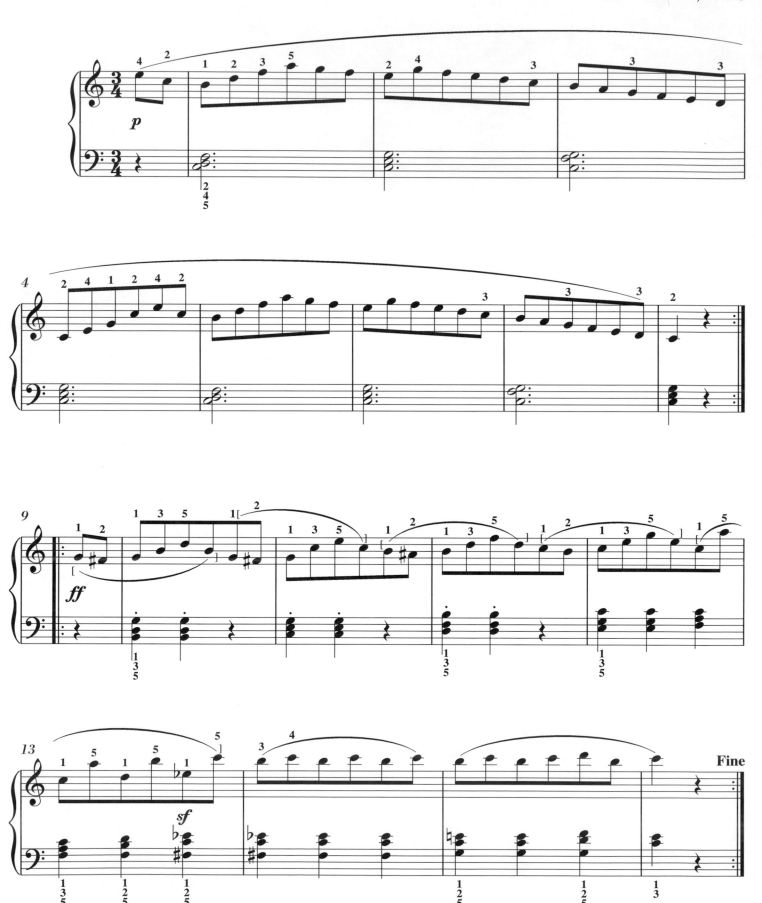

Trio

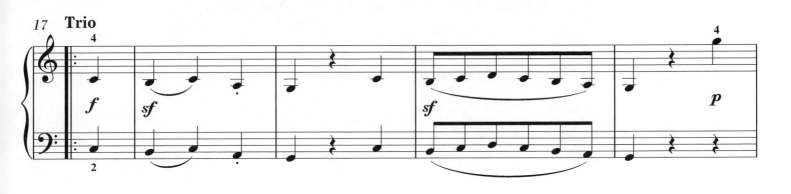

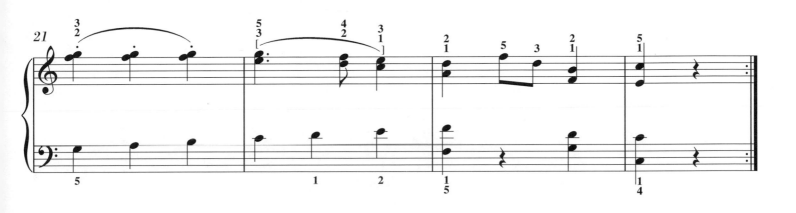

D.C. al Fine
senza repetizione

German Dance in G Major

Ludwig van Beethoven
WoO 8, No. 11

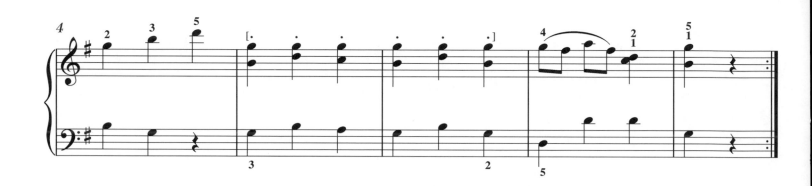

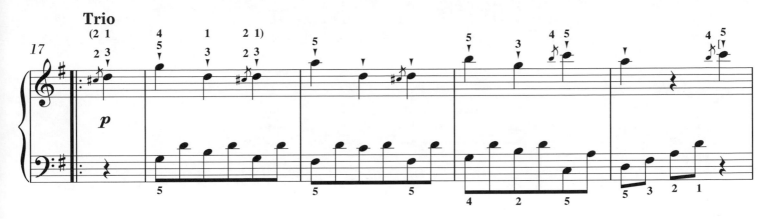

D.C. al Fine
senza repetizione

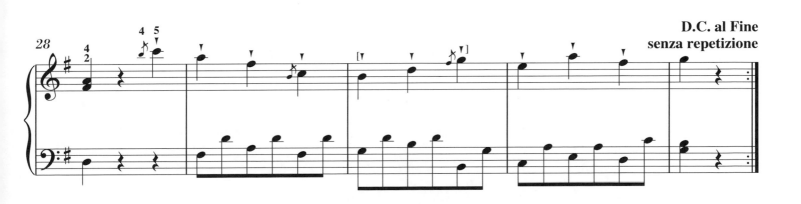

Ländler in D Major

Ludwig van Beethoven
WoO 11, No. 7

Bagatelle in A Minor

Ludwig van Beethoven
Op. 119, No. 9

Contredance in C Major

Ludwig van Beethoven
WoO 14, No. 1

Menuet in B-flat Major

Ludwig van Beethoven
WoO 7, No. 8

Sonatina in G Major

Ludwig van Beethoven
Kinsky-Halm Anh. 5, No. 1

Romanza

Bagatelle in A Major

Ludwig van Beethoven
Op. 119, No. 4

ABOUT THE EDITOR

MATTHEW EDWARDS

Matthew Edwards holds a Doctor of Musical Arts degree in piano performance from the Peabody Conservatory of Music in Baltimore, Maryland, where he studied piano with Robert MacDonald and Robert Weirich.

He was winner of the Grand Prize in the Stravinsky Awards International Competition, and also was awarded First Prize in the Music Teachers National Association National Collegiate Finals. As a pianist, he has appeared throughout the United States as a solo recitalist and collaborative artist, and has performed as guest soloist with several orchestras. He has been hailed by critics for his "...considerable talent...honest musicianship and a formidable technique."

Dr. Edwards has served on the adjunct faculty of several colleges, including the Peabody Conservatory of Music in Baltimore, Maryland. He is currently Assistant Professor of Music at Anne Arundel Community College in Maryland. He is also the rehearsal pianist/coach for the Annapolis Opera, assistant musical director for Opera AACC, and a sought-after collaborative artist in the Mid-Atlantic region. Dr. Edwards frequently presents lectures on piano performance and pedagogy, and has been a featured speaker at the Music Teachers National Association annual conference, the World Piano Pedagogy Conference, and various state conferences throughout the USA. Active also as a composer, his choral, orchestral, and solo piano works have been premiered in Chicago, Salt Lake City, and Baltimore. He is a published composer with Hal Leonard Corporation.